THE PERFECTION OF
AWARENESS

BURT HARDING

Also by Burt Harding:

Hiding in Plain Sight

THE PERFECTION OF
AWARENESS

BURT HARDING

in the garden Publishing

a media company of
WHAT WOULD LOVE DO INT'L LTD

ISBN: 978-1-941351-00-0

Library of Congress data available upon request.

Published by:

IN THE GARDEN PUBLISHING

P.O. Box 752252

Dayton, OH 45475

www.IntheGardenPublishing.com

www.WhatWouldLoveDoIntl.com

CONTENTS

INTRODUCTION

The Perfection of Awareness
Truth is simple.
It is all about Presence.
Unknowable to the intellect,
obvious to the innocent heart.
~ Burt Harding

One day, after a hot August evening satsang, while recalling the several questions people asked about their lives and living it; the many "buts," "what-ifs," and the fears they faced, I had the following realization: I would take a short holiday and let my silence write a book on the most essential heart-knowing of all—the perfection of Awareness in daily life through knowing the difference between thought and Awareness.

The perfection of Awareness is about Presence. Presence cannot be known in the way we know objects and information, as something outside ourselves. From the intellectual point of view, it is utterly unknowable. The paradox is that we do know it, without any doubt at all. In fact, it is the one thing of which we are absolutely certain.

The problem with most seekers is that they want to "get it," as if it is something to be attained. This very attempt is the great block to seeing what already is obvious. We are looking for something that is here—always *now*.

In this book you are pointed in the right direction. Through understanding its message you'll discover the sacred, the radiant beautiful Awareness of Presence everywhere you look.

PART I

1

The Perfection of Awareness

Have you ever asked these questions?

- ☐ I want so much to feel the awareness of Now, but I find it so terribly difficult!
- ☐ It's okay to discuss facing fears and problems in a satsang group where one feels safe, but it is a different story when one is alone in the world and faced with a life-threatening situation.
- ☐ Is there something I am missing when I hear all this spiritual talk? I just don't feel it.
- ☐ I have heard that grace comes unexpectedly. What is grace and how can we trigger it?
- ☐ I want so much to feel peace and clarity in my life!

- ☐ I just want to feel alive and not feel so bound and afraid!
- ☐ I don't feel complete. Am I missing something?

...and hundreds of others!

After years of receiving e-mail questions from all over the world, the recognition has come that the only confusion and uncertainty everyone seems to have revolves around the difference between thought and awareness. There is a vast difference between the two, like night and day, and yet, paradoxically, they complement each other through the oneness of their dual nature.

What became clear to me is that "knowing" the difference between thought and awareness is what tips the scales towards clarity, peace and acceptance.

I can assure you that the understanding of the difference between awareness and thought, and seeing their complementary oneness, brings far more benefit than can be imagined. Here are some benefits from this clarity:

- It will bring clarity, the most important step in understanding.
- It will help you to see what is real as opposed to what is relative and unreal.
- It will bring you peace because the attachment to thought starts to fall away through clarity.
- You will feel more relaxed, comfortable with yourself since effort and struggle is practically diminished.
- You will finally understand what it means to love yourself as the question of self-esteem is forever resolved.
- Fears start to drop by themselves as clarity becomes more established.

- There is a quiet enthusiasm for life and living with a heart open to wonder.
- Self-concern begins to drop until self-consciousness is diminished.
- When questions arise, there is almost an immediate seeing of the answer imbedded in the question itself.
- When problems arise there is no panic or even agitation as understanding between awareness and thought brings detachment.
- The world is seen with new eyes and you begin to also see no separation.
- All seeking to attain, overcome and fix drop away like leaves in autumn.
- There's a continual feeling of release from tension and stress even when presented by worldly activity.
- There's compassion towards others since you see no separation.
- There's a quiet inner excitement about ordinary things and activities. Someone

commented that even washing dishes became a pleasant experience.

- There's an incredible release from mental enslavement and the conditioned nervous system at the realization of what thought is.
- Our greatest fear of emptiness gradually becomes our greatest joy.
- We finally wake up to what is real and lasting.
- Above all, we discover who we are and have always been.

*The first important realization:
There's nothing to find, but
understand "what-is."*

More people than ever are seeking a deeper and more meaningful life aside from the war ravaged world we live in. This seeking, although it is a natural function of the soul reaching for itself, often projects the belief that there's something to find.

This belief is not only a great block to achieving true understanding but also becomes an addiction instead. This obstacle, the belief that there is something to find, can loom so large in our egoic perception of reality that it becomes the source of our frustration, confusion and suffering.

There is absolutely nothing to find, nothing to overcome, nothing to fix, and there's definitely no need for improving anything. What is left is only the clear understanding of what-is here-now.

Once we start clearing our heads of our preconceived notions about spirituality, we can start LOOKING and LISTENING to the miracle of this moment. What we think about this moment has nothing to do with what is real and lasting. In fact, any thought about anything is just a "thought" about something! Do you see the point?

A thought is always *about* something, never the thing itself. We can think, debate and explore love all we like, and we know it to the extent that it is tasted in the moment.

You have probably heard all this before but now is your opportunity to let it sink in. Even as you read this, your mind is making itself up about it. The mind (thought) is always "about it" and therefore cannot experience directly and misses the truth.

I have talked to psychologists, would-be philosophers and intellectuals and they, often miss the point because they base truth on intellectual logic.

Truth is not something to see or even talk about. Truth, the only truth in life, is this moment here-now without any past or future. Truth is available to you right this moment if you can just be still long enough to feel it. Now, as you read this, take a deep breath and sigh deeply, letting go of all physical tension and thought. In your stillness ask, "What am I right now?" and then just FEEL.

All you are and have ever been is NOW-AWARE. It is this Presence that is the truth everyone has been searching for, from the beginning of mankind. This truth is the only Reality that never dies, never changes and is never born—it 'just IS!'

This reality is experienced within us as unconditional love, peace, clarity, oneness and joy. These feelings are NOT emotional qualities, in fact, not qualities at all. They are our true nature as pure presence. If this is your first "looking" experience, it may feel scary and even disappointing because the mind's thinking will exclaim, "Is this IT?"

The mind's conditioned thoughts are so limited that it sees NOW also as being limited, missing completely that NOW is eternal and beyond time and space. It is too vast for the mind to conceive of.

Following this initial realization might come the knowledge that you don't exist as you thought you did, for after all, if you are this vastness of Now, how could you also be a small frail limited person? That's correct, you couldn't be, even though the experience of being the small "you" seems so real.

This Presence does not belong to any person or individual but it is YOU! It is who you truly are.

Now that you have had a small glimpse of what awareness means, let's explore thought, what most people live by 99.9% of their time on earth.

2

The Nature of Thought

In the Bible it states, "In the beginning was the Word, and the Word was made flesh." This is a powerful and significant statement. The 'Word' refers to thought or mind, which is thought itself. Thought is the vehicle by which we imagine, perceive, recall, retain and memorize, to name a few examples.

Thought is NOT Reality but an impression of reality. This impression is an image which, unless it is seen to be merely a thought it becomes "reality" to the perceiver. This so-called reality creates motion in the reactive state known as e-motion (motion of energy).

For instance, if you had an experience as a child of something that frightened you, then every time you think of it, your body will experience that same sensation of fear. The body is cellular memory based on thoughts that have been perceived as real.

In the vast expanse of reality we attract and manifest our vibrational match. If we are vibrating in a place of fear, anger or guilt, we attract and manifest the individuals and circumstances that are vibrating in fear, anger and guilt. This is the universal law of attraction.

Similarly, if we are vibrating in a place of joy and love we also manifest our match. If you meet a lot of people who are often complaining or angry, then you need to look at your inner dialogue (pattern of thinking).

If you find that people are being nice to you, then that's what you are manifesting through your vibrations. There is no good or bad in the world, which is hard for most people to understand. Truly, it is only thought that makes it so, as Shakespeare wrote, "There is no good or bad, only thinking makes it so."

3

Everything is Thought (Mind)

Here is a great truth—everything you see, and for that matter, everything in the universe, emanates from your mind. Try to feel the reality of this incredible yet true statement. You do not have to think about it, just observe how much you are controlled by your thoughts. Every feeling you have starts out as a thought, which becomes a feeling only when it is not seen as such.

Oftentimes we confuse thought with our heart or intuition when in reality it began as subtle fear or doubt that only afterward became strong feeling. Any "awakened" individual will tell you that everything you see that seems real in the world—animals, worms, minerals, vegetables, your body—is a manifestation of your mind.

This might seem hard to take initially, but as you read on keeping your heart open, you will realize the truth in it. If you but relax and start looking into the heart of stillness, you will start to have a deeper understanding of how everything you "know" is thought appearing as the world.

It is like watching television and being immersed in the show to the point that you identify completely with the character in the story. At the time of watching, the show appears real and brings up an emotional response, yet it is all just a play of mind.

I remember many times that I have gotten emotionally involved with movies that were acted so long ago that most of the actors are long dead, and yet they seemed very real while I was watching. The suggestive power of thought is the strongest power in the world.

Most of the feelings we have are NOT real, simply because they emerge from thought (imagination). Most people confuse reality with their own thinking. Most have lost the ability to feel with their heart, and as a result, experience immense emotional suffering.

The body is a magnificent and powerful illustration of the immense and staggering power of thought that is manifested into seeming reality. The form of the human body is evolved to its present stage through billions of years of evolution (Word made flesh).

When you refer to your body, what do you say? Don't you say "my body?" Have you ever asked yourself, "Who is this 'my' you are referring to?" You say "it's mine," as if you own it. Yet, who owns it?

This is an example of how we confuse thought with awareness. It takes awareness just to see and feel the body in the first place; and in saying "it is mine,'" it is clear (to an objective viewer) that you are NOT the body, but something you believe you own.

4

You are Spirit (Awareness)

The question may arise, "Why is thought needed if we are already spirit?"

Spirit manifests as thought just as your body casts a shadow, but is NOT the shadow. Similarly, spirit creates thought out of itself, just like a spider weaves a web from itself. It is this creation of form-body that creates our ability to recognize our own true nature as spirit.

Spirit is pure awareness and is therefore unborn. The awareness through which you experience life is not "your" awareness, but Awareness itself, appearing as "you." When you think that you are merely a body/mind mechanism, then you suffer with thoughts such as...

I am not enough...

I should be better...

I must improve...

There is something lacking, but don't know what...

I must be missing something...

I don't feel good-enough as I am...

There is something wrong with me...

I must have more of money, success, power to make up for my lack...

These beliefs, which are often deep set, are not often questioned except through deep inquiry, and so remain imbedded in our belief-system masquerading as reality.

5

Evolution of Consciousness

In the first stages of the evolution of human consciousness, the simplest consciousness is directed primarily by survival instinct.

Expressions at this level are crude and coarse, communication is rough and overbearing. After much passage of time and experience, self-consciousness emerges and we are finally able to look at ourselves. Most people on the planet at this time are in the self-conscious stage.

Self-consciousness generates a strong ego and also the ability to see what works and doesn't work. At this time of self-consciousness, we start to see the futility of war and violence. In the simpler survival consciousness stage, we actually believe that war is essential.

Our consciousness is now moving deeper, beyond the surface level. The more we recognize the intelligence of life (Source-Spirit), the more we move inward towards the center. This "movement" toward the center progresses as each habitual way of thinking collapses. Thought (belief, viewpoint, conditioning) can only shift into greater seeing when thought is seen for what it actually is—a thought!

On the surface level of thinking we assume that what we think is actually reality. This belief alone contributes to immense suffering, confusion and inner pain. When we move into the center of the spiral we are awakened more and more to what is real and lasting. We do not stop thinking, but we simply see thoughts as thoughts; in other words, we do not believe them wholesale anymore. Becoming more and more aware of the vast field of awareness behind and beyond our thoughts creates peace of mind.

The paradox is this—the evolution of consciousness only seems to happen to us while we are in our conditioned state of mind, but in reality, Awareness is never touched by anything we do or feel.

6

Thought is Always "about it"

Here are some facts about thought. Thoughts are always born in duality, such as right/wrong, good/bad, black/white, up/down, and so forth, and are accordingly judgmental.

In reality, there is only awareness, which is always pure, non-dual and whole. But thought can't see what-is; it can only think about it. For example, you can read books about love, write poems, and sing love songs, but until you feel love in your heart, you don't know love.

Thoughts are all "about" love and are not love itself. Thought cannot experience directly and cannot feel except through relatively coarse surface emotion. The mind processes surface emotion as feeling, and if suffering is deep then it calls it deep feeling; it has lost touch with feeling from the heart and therefore, even truth evades it.

7

Awareness Just "IS"

Awareness is open to anything and everything. It doesn't "know," because by definition, knowing must be from the past. Awareness is totally alive, fresh and new NOW—empty of preconceptions.

Awareness sees no other state, and therefore does not suffer separation. It says "yes" to what is here and now, and never resists. Awareness accepts everything and holds on to nothing. It is unconditional love. Perception is always conditioned and conditional, but awareness is not and cannot be.

Awareness is aliveness and the ONLY real "thing" there is. It is by the grace of awareness that we think and emote, but it itself is free of thought.

There is no opposite of awareness, yet thought exists only in opposites. Thought by its very nature divides and classifies, resists and excludes.

Have you ever noticed that right after experiencing deep love, feeling alive and inwardly rich, thought tries to take over and try to own it, bringing in fear of rejection and fear of commitment?

Thought is limited and depends on awareness for its existence; yet awareness does not depend on thought. Just as awareness, unchanging presence, is the sole reality, so is thought a shadow that appears as the world of form and matter.

Awareness is the source of all. It is unborn and eternal. It is Oneness. It is love. It is whole. It was never created and therefore has no beginning or end. It is useless to try to figure out the immensity of Awareness (now), yet thought keeps trying to do just that.

This "thinking-about-it" only creates more fog and confusion and blocks the very simplicity of what-is. This is why surrendering and silencing the mind can yield such incredible benefits toward awakening consciousness.

Awareness is infinite intelligence itself acting through us, and yet it is us.

We are that Source and there is only IT. Awareness is free, spontaneous, open, fresh, innocent, alive and totally here. On the other hand, thought is reactionary, based on memory, projection, habit and survival. It is divisive, manipulative and strategic.

8

Your Feelings about

Thought & Awareness

As we explore awareness and thought, do you find yourself judging thought as wrong and awareness as right? This is the nature of the mind— it can't help judging everything. Therefore, if this is the nature of the mind, then is it wrong?

The important thing is to see the mind's action as simply what the mind does and NOT who you are. Your nature is Awareness, which uses the mind for the purpose of promoting survival.

Once you start seeing this clearly, you'll allow the mind to do what it does and not identify with it. This is how you awaken to your true nature. You don't do anything to accomplish awakening, but simply ALLOW yourself to see what is real and lasting which is awareness (your Presence).

Seekers have the idea that enlightenment means acquiring a constantly aware state and a totally quieted mind. This is nonsense. Nothing changes after awakening but the understanding of what is real and lasting. Awareness is unborn and unchanging.

It is through this unchanging awareness that you were able to experience the changes in your body and personality ever since you were a baby in the crib. Everything in "you" has changed, except the very awareness you are. Awareness is your true nature and you can enjoy NOT avoiding or controlling the mind, but including it (and seeing it for what it is).

The mind is a wonderful servant when it knows its place. You cannot practice awareness because it is always there, your natural state. Therefore, whenever the mind "acts up," simply be aware of it and see that it is NOT who you are.

The mind is reactive and any unresolved fears from the past will keep popping up. When you become aware of their "popping," then the very awareness of that, clearly seeing the difference between thought and awareness, will automatically resolve them. This is how healing takes place. You don't stop thought—it is impossible.

Allow the thought to arise and know, "It is only a thought."

9

Seeing Truth is Effortless

Just stop running away from it. There is no work to be done—all is effortless. What is necessary to do is to know the difference between thought and awareness. The clearer you are about them, the more you can allow them to blend and be one.

For instance, let's assume that the cast shadow that follows your body is fearful to you and you try to avoid it. You run and it follows, keeping pace with you. You run faster and faster, becoming tired, but it is still there. Then, utterly exhausted and prostrate on the ground, you realize it is just a harmless shadow. What happens next?

Nothing changes, but your understanding has freed you from the fear. The shadow is still there but who cares? The shadow can be seen as the thoughts of your mind. If you attempt to control them or get rid of them, they become even more real to you. It is only when you see them as they actually are—just thoughts—that the fears stop and you are healed.

Thoughts are harmless unless you believe they are real, and then they can be extremely dangerous. Destructive emotions and phobias, deep depression, suicidal tendencies and the like are nothing more than thoughts which have been believed and thus made real.

All the above may seem abstract and mentally heavy. It is always a bit heavy mentally when we are confronted by something new to the mind.

However, the important thing to realize is this— either this is true or it isn't! I can tell you that this is definitely true and can be easily recognized if you allow yourself to start becoming aware of your thoughts.

Allow yourself to watch your thoughts from moment to moment. For instance, observe yourself making any simple choice (making a thought real is an unconscious choice). With direct exploration comes direct knowledge of the truth. Inquiring into what the mind is telling you without judging it to be bad or good, true or false, can be an extremely rich unfolding.

10

Unchanging Presence

Take a moment to be still, preferably in an environment where there is silence and no phones, crowds, honking cars and so on. Just be still and LOOK (witness, observe, see) how, in fact, you are just awareness.

Explore the question, "What am I?" and inquire into what you are at this moment. Your name, form and conditioning exist in your past, but in this silent and empty moment, what are you? Feel it out through a few moments of fear that will naturally arise.

Soon you will glimpse that you are indeed the presence of awareness. This aware presence has no beginning or end. There has never been a time when you were not aware that you existed. In time you will discover that this awareness is truly joy, clarity, freedom, love and happiness. Soon you will find that YOU JUST ARE!

Once you accept this inevitable and choiceless truth, you are awake and free. The mind will continue to do what it does, and you can even enjoy its sometimes dark, sometimes frivolous exploits with the cosmic humor.

11

Dealing with Emotions

By now, you have learned that emotions are thoughts that are believed to be real and therefore act as sensation in the body. Emotions mean motion of energy in the body through belief. No matter how you feel emotionally, no matter how desperate or unhappy you become, there is always the watcher witnessing what is going on ready to assist if we turn to it. This watcher is your Awareness.

Awareness is unconditional love and despite self-hate or self-destruction, Awareness remains steadfast and unyielding. It is only the mind that suffers and creates fear—such is unknown to Awareness (Presence).

Now, armed with this knowledge, there are three steps you could take that will bring healing. In fact, the real transformation happens when we can face the fear of inner emptiness and darkness with equanimity knowing we are the living presence. Sometimes this living presence is known as I AM.

Did you know that the fastest transformation happens when you accept your darkest moments and invite the light? To repeat, this is our greatest opportunity...

Our greatest opportunity is to go into the deepest, darkest places within the human experience and find the Light. The Light is inherent within our own innate Awareness, and our ability to choose.

12

From Darkness into Light

Just as darkness is unconsciousness, so is awareness light. Here are the three steps to take in turning the past into the light of this moment through Awareness.

1. The moment you find yourself in a sad, unhappy, angry or dark mood, just acknowledge it immediately by saying something like, "There is a feeling of darkness inside this body." Then take a deep breath followed by a slow exhaling sigh.

2. Sit down and observe the sensation in the body without labeling it as fear, anger or depression. Just see it as a dark color sensation in the body. Locate the area experiencing this sensation the most. If any story arises like, "poor me," or "I

wish I could ring their necks," or "why did this happen to me," and so on, then become aware that there's a story happening and repeat, "Story! Story!" Keep watching that location and its sensation like a scientist looking through a microscope.

3. It's imperative that you are a detached observer of the whole sensation without the need to change it or overcome it. You are unconditionally loving yourself during this process of acceptance. This dark sensation will start to move inevitably as you study it without judgment. When this darkness starts to lighten up, then it is clear that it is healing. If it becomes as light as light blue or golden yellow or pink, then you know it is healed.

This process could take anywhere between 1 minute to 15 minutes. If you were to do this every time you felt heavy, soon you'll recognize the difference between Awareness and thought. When you bring Awareness into a strong thought (belief), you'll start noticing the difference between thought and Awareness. After a few times, the distinction between them becomes so clear that you'll understand their interaction.

You are a human being. Just as thought (mind) is your human part, so is Awareness your Being part. When you start seeing how it all works together, you'll integrate human and being into wholeness. You will feel and live in wholeness.

13

Distinguishing Between

Thought & Awareness

THOUGHT	AWARENESS
Duality thinks in opposites	Oneness
Can't see only thinks about it	Whole
Conditioned past	No past knowledge
Always in the process of becoming	Empty from preconceptions
Classifies, resists, excludes	Includes all, says yes to life

It knows from memory & projection	Alive, fresh, new
Self-fulfilling prophecies	Energy & core of essence
Tries to get someplace	Unconditioned, formless
Mechanical, habitual, patterned	Unconditional love
It judges	Spontaneous
Lives in past and future	Lives fully now
Human	Being
Time	Now

Thought depends on Awareness; Awareness does not depend on thought. Awareness makes thought possible.

14

Questions and Answers

It's okay to discuss facing fears and problems in a satsang place where one feels safe, but it is a different story when one is faced with a life-threatening situation.

The wonderful thing about knowing the difference between thought and awareness is that it releases you from all fear. For instance, what would you say is the greatest fear of mankind? Isn't it the fear of death?

Now, what if you realize that your true nature is Awareness, which is unborn and therefore undying, would you still have the same fear?

Something happened to me in May, 2006, that further amplified what I am saying here. For many years I admired the teachings of Bhagavan Ramana Maharshi who taught me, through his teachings, that true life is eternal and goes on despite the death of the body.

In the beginning of May, I became sick with a very high fever. After a few days the fever persisted, reaching a 105 degree temperature. Sivia became concerned and called paramedics.

At this time my left leg swelled up twice the size of the other, my back had lesions in black, blue, red and when pressed, liquid oozed from them. I was as pale as a sheet of paper and could not stand much less walk. I lost a lot of weight as I couldn't eat without wanting to throw up. In other words, I was dying.

I knew I was dying and didn't want to alarm Sivia with that affirmation. I accepted my forthcoming death and even surrendered to it.

As the ambulance reached the hospital and I was wheeled into the hospital something strange happened—everything disappeared—the nurses, doctors, patients including myself. Sivia became part of a bright warm loving presence.

At that moment there was no Burt or anyone else—just that warm loving Light and I knew I was IT! There was no Burt anymore but this Light which included everyone in it.

When the experience subsided and the doctors approached me they looked concerned, putting me in isolation since they thought it was a rare disease I contracted from a foreign land. As one doctor after another questioned me, I smiled but had not much strength to speak.

I was in absolute bliss, so much so, in fact that Sivia had an "experience" just being with me. The doctors and nurses were baffled but intrigued both by my appearance and blissful presence. I couldn't help feeling wonderful.

The doctor approached me and said with a serious face, "This is very serious. I will come back later after some tests."

When he told me this, I couldn't keep a serious face but had to smile at his words filled with so much concern. I was kept in isolation for 16 hours while Sivia slept on the floor of the small windowless room that we were kept in. I was given IV treatment. Sivia, knowing I was happy, was not concerned anymore and asked me what had happened.

Well, to make a long story short, the next couple of days a doctor said that it was a serious case of blood poisoning. A few days later (six to be exact), I was released and healed. The doctor was amazed at the quick recovery. I replied that the healing happened because there was no thought of fear.

Is there something I am missing? When I hear all this spiritual talk, I don't feel it.

You are not missing anything, but because you believe you are a memory (name, form, education, culture, nationality, religion and conditioning) then you believe you are missing something. You are a human who has forgotten the eternal being. Keep on exploring the difference between thought and Awareness until you see clearly the difference, and also their completion in each other.

You seem so convinced all that is necessary is knowing the difference between thought and Awareness. Why is that?

If you discover for yourself, through stillness and silence, the difference between thought and Awareness, then what else do you need to know?

You can literally toss aside all religion, philosophy, psychology, metaphysics and new age teachings, for you will know, beyond any doubt, who and what you are.

After all, what is the greatest discovery you can make in life? Isn't it knowing who and what you are? And, this knowing in your heart without question, that you are unborn and therefore undying, is not that filled with peace and fearlessness?

When you are freed from your fears then there is no longer a search for peace, security and safety in life. You will have found it in this very *moment*.

How does grace take place?

Grace is the emptiness of NOW if we are willing to empty our thought processes for just a moment, becoming open to grace. It is grace that will bring the full recognition of who and what you are— without any doubt!!

Why have most people forsaken the inner knowledge of Awareness when it is so immediate?

It is *because* it is so immediate (and all there is) that it is missed. For instance, you look at a tree and say it is beautiful but miss the very Awareness of it that made it possible to experience it.

Why does thought play a major role in life when it is an effect rather than a cause?

The effect is all we ever experience simply because we are the cause. The cause is the source that creates everything out of itself. By the same token of Awareness, we see only what we are aware of and never turn the Awareness back on itself and say, "Here's awareness doing the looking and experiencing."

When I "get it" after reading this book, do I receive all the benefits mentioned automatically?

You will receive them if you recognize the difference through following the process of looking at what-is (as discussed in the three steps). Reading this book alone doesn't cut it. It is imperative that you use what you read.

How do I recognize the Truth?

There is only One Truth and that is Awareness. When you start recognizing its enormity, power, its infallibility and eternal nature, then you will start knowing that it is YOU you are seeing. It is here, which is recognition.

Is there some practice I must do to realize that what I am reading is real and earnest?

Yes, reflect in moments of stillness and silence, asking yourself, "What am I right now?" Soon, as you become empty, you will start to see that all you are is just here-now-Awareness.

What is Presence?

Presence is the fact that all you are is this Awareness here-now, and nothing else (except thoughts you accumulated from the past which are just memory). Look around you and tell me what you are right now as you read this.

Presence is the all-encompassing Awareness of all that is.

I know the difference between thought and Awareness but I do not exhibit the benefits you mentioned?

Understanding must come from the heart and NOT thought. There is the idea that the mind (thought) understands. It doesn't, it can only know "about it," but never a direct experience of it. To realize that you don't understand it through thought alone opens the heart.

What does understanding mean?

It is a paradox. It means literally that there's nothing specific to understand but to see the difference between thought and Awareness like you see the difference between your body and its shadow.

Understanding is really seeing with innocent eyes knowing that there's nothing to figure out. If it is a mental activity then it's a thought. If it's seeing something just as it is, then it's Awareness. For example, look at the tree in front of you but do not call it a tree...just look and see it as it actually is without a label, judgment or preference.

You'll see it as it actually is. Then look at your Awareness without being aware of anything and see how everything is Awareness and that's why it appears to exist.

If you "get this" then you understand.

Why does it take so long to live the life of Truth even when we understand the difference between thought and Awareness?

It seems to take a long time because the Awareness is still in the background and the thought of it is still playing its major role in your belief system.

What can I expect after reading this book?

Any expectations you have will be a setback to what is "supposed" to happen.

How can I not have expectations and beliefs?

You weren't told not to have expectations and beliefs, they are the nature of thought. Just see the difference between thought and Awareness, that's all.

Once this difference is clear, it will guide you. Awareness is the only reality we have while thought emerges from it. They work together for final awakening. A thought can NEVER be real because it is an effect of Source. Source is Awareness!

Am I to deny all my thoughts then?

Who said you should deny anything? Any denial is a lack of seeing what-is, as it actually is!

This seems difficult to see beyond the thoughts and just see Awareness?

Who asked you to see beyond the thoughts? Thoughts are thoughts and Awareness is what produces them. In Truth, all you are is Awareness playing with thoughts. You are only asked to see what is real here—now.

I get confused when I start watching.

It is because you are still not seeing what-is, but only what you think you should see.

I am so confused, what should I do?

Just relax and forget the whole thing for now. Then, when your mind is refreshed ask yourself who was confused. It was only the thought that gets confused. Awareness can never become confused because it JUST IS!

How can I be Awareness when I am not even clear what it is?

You are Awareness whether you believe it or not. You have never been anything else. The thought that you have to learn about Awareness is like trying to teach your eyes to see and your ears to hear.

Awareness is all there is and the reason you can see these words is because you are AWARE of them. Awareness is all there is and it appears as mind, thought and emotions. If you can find moments when there is no thought and emotions then just look and see how peaceful, beautiful and alive you feel.

You say Awareness is love, peace, joy and happiness. I don't get it. Can you explain?

What happens when you are fully relaxed without a thought in your head about doing this or that? You find yourself happy, right?

Unhappiness, suffering, depression, anger, and so on are simply conditioned responses from habitual thinking that you are not good enough, that something is wrong with you and that you are not love. So, you either seek love or control (power) to make up for a lack that never existed.

When I am happy and feeling really good, am I being Awareness then?

There's never a time when you are not Awareness. However, you forget about being Awareness because you focus on what you are being aware of.

For instance, if someone called you a good-for-nothing then you could mull over it and get either angry or depressed because you became aware of the words as if they were real. You are always aware but, because you take everything personally. you place Awareness into a thought-form instead.

How can I know when I am being fully aware?

You don't, because you are too happy to bother. It is like the boy playing ball tossing it back and forth against the wall and can't even hear his mother when she calls him. Finally she comes over and finds him enthralled playing ball. She asks him, "Are you having fun dear?" The boy pauses long enough to answer meanwhile losing the edge of fun in answering the question.

When you are being fully aware you are NOT self-concerned and so you feel connection with what-is, which is—love of the moment. At that moment of love, there is no one to know if one is being aware or not.

Why do you feel that it is the most important realization?

It cuts down all the esoteric extraneous details and gives you ways to realize the truth and thus living a normal natural life. When you accept your true nature as Awareness, then you'll also accept your humanness as thought and its illusions.

Everything having to do with daily life is thought and it is NOT as real as we make it out to be. This realization will free us from trying to save the world and changing people's thoughts and other effortful attempts at changing things.

You finally relax knowing, without a doubt, that everything is okay just as it is. All you do then is LOVE—love everything and everyone in a very natural way because there is not a thing that is not Awareness in appearance.

Everything is part of you and is YOU!

Are there other terms you can use besides the words 'Awareness' and 'thought' that can make it more understandable?

Look up the list I made describing Awareness and its opposite, thought. You will see more of its many levels. For example, let's take the word Awareness as totally NOW. Then compare it to the word "thought" as TIME.

Now we have the two words Now and Time instead of Awareness and Thought. These terms can make it simpler to grasp. For example, let's compare the city of Bombay, India to Vancouver, Canada. When we are having dinner here in Vancouver, in Bombay they are having breakfast. The time is totally opposite. Therefore time is always changing according to space/time continuum.

Now, let's assume you are having that dinner and recall that in Bombay they are having breakfast. Isn't it happening right here and now? So, while time creates a gap and change, yet NOW is always NOW everywhere in the universe. Time is illusory because it presents past and future rather than NOW.

The future may be called tomorrow or next week or next year but it is all a concept because you cannot show it here-now. It only exists in time, which is relative to the conceptual mind.

However, if you are anxious about tomorrow and the anxiety is happening presently, then what is happening is that the story concerning tomorrow is causing the anxiety.

Now suppose you dispense with the story for a moment and stick with the feeling of anxiety (without calling it anxiety)? What happens?

You will still feel the sensation of anxiety without its story so that you have brought it closer to home. When you embrace this feeling called anxiety without its story and label, you are left with just a neutral sensation.

As you allow it, breathe into it, and even embrace it, what happens is that your body relaxes into it and, before you know it, all anxiety has melted and you are free to face whatever tomorrow brings with greater peace and equanimity.

Time is relative as explained in Einstein's theory of relativity. NOW is real, and the only reality there is. Now contains everything that happens in the present time, but NOW itself is timeless. NOW is a container of everything that happens in the present, but is NOT the present.

Once you understand this simple explanation you have grasped that this Now is aware-space known as Presence. Time is known as thought. Through your inner guidance and open-heart, you will discover that the two (both time and thought) work as one.

Once this is clear to the point of seeing, its obviousness then you will start to live it. Once you are living it, you are living Truth. It is a life of ease, peace, love and joy.

There's something I am not quite clear on—

do you mean to say that only NOW is real and time is not real?

Let's define what it means to be real or unreal. Reality is what-is in this moment. This is even common sense to see the Now as the real, for after all, when can anything happen, appear or be experienced other than now? Can anything appear 'not-now?'

This question is absurd. When tomorrow is mentioned, can you show me tomorrow? When you live in thoughts of yesterday or tomorrow, aren't they in your mind only? How can thoughts be reality?

It is true that they may fee' real in your body, especially if you recall some past tragedy, experience or memory, but then it is strictly emotional.

Emotional feeling is a thought, memory, recollection made real even though it is history. In this context anything that is based on time is conceptual (in the realm of thought only). It is in this case that we say it is "not real." It is happening in your mind, which lives in linear time and therefore is not reality but something that happened (history).

The term unreal does not mean it is not happening in your emotional body, it simply means it is not reality, it is NOT Truth. It is also unreal because if you do not think about it, where is it?

When you are happy, relaxed, peaceful, joyous, contented and feeling safe and secure, it simply means that you are here—now. This *now* itself is joy and love. Similarly, when you are depressed, unhappy, angry, worried and generally caught in your mind, this is termed unreal because it is all conceptual and NOT Reality.

When you are living now, you feel alive and happy. However, what is interesting to know and recognize is this—that reality has no opposite. This means that reality sees no duality of good and bad, right and wrong or even should or shouldn't. It sees only what-is without labeling or judging.

So, no matter what happens in the moment, even if it's a thought, is immediately accepted and embraced just as a thought and nothing more. If anxiety or some tragic memory arises in your mind, then it is seen for what it is and experienced in the body just exactly as it is—a thought! This immediate awareness and acceptance alters the effects from the past thought automatically and effortlessly.

This effortless living happens when there is a full intuitive grasp of the difference between thought and Awareness (between now and time).

Is that what is meant by being "awake" or "asleep?"

Yes! Being awake means being fully present with whatever is happening without judging, comparing, analyzing or conceptualizing. Being awake does not mean denying any concepts that arise, it means seeing anything that is not there now as a concept and it's okay.

Concepts are not wrong, they are just concepts. In reality, there is no wrong or right but only LOVE, which means, there is only NOW! Now and Love are synonymous. If you become still and feel this NOW, you will recognize the automatic love in it.

On the other hand, when you get caught in self-defense, protection of your ego, or take things personally, then this is termed being asleep to your true nature of pure nowness.

Being asleep means being unconscious of your true nature which is now. In other words, you think of yourself as a person (personal) and that's why there is unconsciousness.

Doesn't everyone think of themselves as a person?

Yes, and that's why the world is such a mess filled with greed, war, violence, hate, separation, bigotry and guilt. When you realize that all you are is this presence of Awareness, here and now, you are free.

Ask yourself right now, "Who are you?" and you will feel dumbfounded and no answer will emerge— and do you know why?

Simply because there is no person behind it! There is only the presence of Awareness eternally here and now. The person believes that the Awareness is his or hers but in truth Awareness *just is* and although it appears as the aliveness of over six billion people on this earth, it is One Awareness.

There is only this Oneness known as love. It is only when you realize this Oneness that you also realize how asleep the average mind is.

I was in your satsang when you asked me, 'What are you right now?' and I didn't know what to say, however, even in my dumbfoundedness there was a glimmer that I am not a person. For a moment I felt I was everyone. I didn't feel like saying anything, it was wonderful beyond words. The feeling stayed with me after satsang and even into the next day. Then at work facing daily problems the knowing was gone and was back to being a person again. Could you explain how to retain it?

The very attempt at trying to retain it becomes the block to it. There is nothing to retain, however there was the belief that you had attained something and then lost it. You cannot lose the natural state, it is who you really are. The problem is this—that you have invested so much energy in being a person that the slightest setback draws you back to what is familiar.

So, you didn't lose anything, you simply fell back into habit-thinking and believing.

So how can I live from it all the time?

You are still believing that you are your thoughts, beliefs and mindset. There is still the attachment to the past you. Just find out moment-to-moment if that is truly the case. You don't try to live from it all the time, IT is living you all the time but the habit-attachment (ego) says that IT is something you'd like to live from. So, you have created two of you—the habit-attachment and the IT or true state of you.

How can I live daily life doing business transactions and dealing with people when everyone believes they are a person?

You are still buying into the deception of habit. The main thing is to live from what you have discovered to be true. Truth is what matters—it matters simply because it is true. When you start living honestly then you live with integrity and love. What better combination is there in living daily life, business life or relationship life then living with integrity and honesty?

Keep inquiring at least a few times a day, "What am I?" and if any fears arise from the possibility that you are not a person as most people believe, then ask yourself, "Have I ever been a person?"

It is only scary because we think we have lost something, but have you?

Can I reach a point where I can live daily life from this knowing?

Ask yourself this question now and see for yourself. Knowing is not something attained— knowing is a recognition of how things are and have always been. This recognition is up to you and how much you want what is true and lasting in your life.

If you truly want to be free, happy, open, peaceful and inwardly secure and fearless then just keep listening to your heart. People who believe they are an ego (person) are defensive, easily angered, afraid, prone to frustration, confusion and continual fear. These are not bad feelings, they are just ignorance of one's true being nature. This is why the founder of Psycho-Synthesis Assagiola said, "95% of our energy is spent protecting, defending and maintaining our self-image and it's all imagination."

A person is just a self-image and doesn't see what is obvious. All you need is a sincere drive for what is true and ask, "Who am I?" and then see how there is no answer to it simply because there is no person here and now, it only exists as memory. Are you memory or just a living pulsating being here and now that is aware?

Can't I be both a human and being living now?

That's the whole point. Once you know that you are NOT the memory, then you accept it fully and compassionately. It is like having a coat you love, are you the coat or is it something you have and love? Similarly with having a mind/body organism—they are a unique expression of you but are not YOU.

Nothing changes through this recognition except becoming free from fears and time-consciousness. You will function more energetically and efficiently without having to be one-upmanship in your business or relationships.

There is absolutely nothing to compare with the joy and freedom that emerges from the KNOWING that you are pure Awareness here and now, yet having thoughts, dreams and time as a play of the life you are. It is this recognition of the difference between thought and Awareness that integrates you fully as a human being. People will notice your kindness and love nature but to you it is merely being your-Self!

I have read that a teacher can transmit the truth to a student. Is that true?

Transmission happens when the student listens well and feels ready to undo his/her ego. The power of the teacher is not his/her words but the Silence that can be transmitted from the heart. Thus, when the heart is open to receive, then the recognition of the teacher is experienced directly by the student.

In Truth there is no teacher or student for truth is One, therefore, what is transmitted is the connection that the student feels at the moment with the teacher. The teacher cannot do anything, it is all up to the student.

The greater the recognition of the teacher with his/her cosmic knowing, the greater will be the transmission when the student surrenders through listening and openness.

What is the function of the teacher if there are no people and nothing to give out as knowledge?

The teacher merely talks about what is here-now. He/she keeps talking until the student starts to listen beyond the words. The waking up happens when one realizes there was nothing to learn, nothing to overcome and nothing to improve but SEE what is obvious here and now.

This SEEING of NOW as all there is in its pure aware-presence is the ultimate Truth. Once you see clearly that there never was or can be anything else that is real then you are free.

Once you are free what else is there?

This knowing of freedom despite circumstances and happenings in the world around you is so glorious and joyous that even talking about it seems blasphemous. Truth lived is paradise gained.

Words are necessary until they are no longer necessary.

I understand that what keeps me from living the truth is resistance and identification with the past memory of me. Is there a way of rising above this resistance and identification?

The wonderful thing about knowing who you are, which is Aware-Presence, is that there is nothing to do, overcome, attain or improve...but just listen. Now, the trick is, how does one listen?

Listening means being vigilant to the egoic need to live in time, to protect itself, to maintain its existence and to struggle in seeking itself someplace else rather than now-here. I assume you know all this, so the simplest thing is to be immediately aware the moment resistance arises and just say, "Thank you for making me aware of this resistance."

That's it! Nothing else is needed. The key thing is this—you listen by recognizing that you hardly ever listen. You don't stop identifying because it won't work but just LISTEN (vigilant Awareness) to how you're identifying with practically everything.

This very seeing of resistance, not listening and identifying with an ego is itself enough to make you realize how much needless suffering they bring. Once you see the needless suffering then they automatically drop—as simple as that! After all, who wants to suffer?

I watched some of your video clips on YouTube and noticed the importance of unconditional love. I find that even the thought of unconditional love is way over my head. Is there a simple way to start?

Unconditional love, believe it or not, is your natural state. It isn't difficult to love unconditionally but it depends upon your level of

Awareness. Start with yourself, after all, the highest form of unconditional love is towards yourself.

Become aware of your fears, regrets, guilt, shame, anger and egoic preoccupation and then take three steps:

a) Acknowledge the feeling in your body (all negative emotions are felt in the body).
b) Take a deep breath and sigh completely relaxing the body into that feeling.
c) Say, "Thank you" for making me aware of it and strong enough to accept it.

That's it! This is the highest unconditional love towards yourself, it is true compassion even though you might be down on yourself, yet you accept it as a learning tool. This first step might be all you really need. Soon you will find unconditionally loving others the same way you did towards you.

Does anything happen to the brain when we recognize the difference between thought and Awareness?

We are not stuck with the intelligence that is inherited and neither is it dependent on the years we have lived. A brain shift happens when we start recognizing what is true, which is Awareness, and the greater the realization, the greater the brain shift and its capacity to know and understand.

We do not understand by the brain but through consciousness, however, the brain expands to accommodate the greater awareness of reality.

Alterations in consciousness are actually visible in people becoming more aware of their true nature as they undergo shifts restructuring the brain and its chemistry becoming kinder with childlike innocence and simplicity along with a marked degree in intelligence. It was visible with Albert Einstein and other advanced beings.

I have experienced near death and later became aware that it was what I needed to break me free from my 'sleep' pattern. Do you know anything about that?

People usually go through transformation and become more of themselves because the potential inherent within them expands when released.

In near-death cases, you hear experiencers admit that what happened to them was what they needed, that it was somehow "ordered" by the Source that we are.

Another thing that happens is that Awareness is released from its confinement to just thought.

What is meant by Awareness release?

We are made up of time and "now." In other words, we are creations of evolution and time. Thus, in order to live in the world, we are dictated by time and by instincts such as survival and adaptation. As a result of this, we miss the very simple knowing of who we are and become confined to thought. Our everyday life becomes imprisoned by thought—everything we do involves "thinking about-it" or analysis, comparison, judgment, figuring-out, logic and so on.

This is okay when we are dealing with daily practical living but, as a result of this confinement; we lose touch with who we are. We lose the truth of our being and so end up unhappy, miserable, dissatisfied, unclear, confused, materialistic and driven for power and control. Our heart, as a result of too much mind, becomes drowned in its capacity to love, laugh and be free in its spontaneous expression of living. Suffering is created by mind and the heart becomes blocked.

Also, when we start seeking answers to life, we do it also intellectually which further exacerbates the situation and so go through a long process of "doing" instead of "being."

Picture the sky and the clouds—the sky is our Being and the mind is the clouds. When we see the difference between thought and Awareness, we see that the sky is Awareness and the clouds are thoughts.

Despite a cloudy dismal dreary dark day, the sky is above the clouds and still shines in its freedom and light. We see how both need each other and yet differently. This realization of this obvious fact becomes "The Awareness Release." We release Awareness from its bondage to thought, not by removing thought, but by seeing the truth of the situation.

Isn't thought essential for living?

Without thought there is no world as we know it and no brain to accommodate consciousness-awareness. The point is not changing anything or even improving anything, but SEEING what is real (Source) rather than its result.

Awareness is eternal and it is the One Truth, whereas thought is the result from awareness. Yet the two are inseparable. It is in knowing the difference, and yet, how they are both one that we release Awareness from its hold by the mind. The great mistake is making thought our primary goal.

If the moment is timeless and yet contains the entire present time, is it possible to contain both past and future?

The timeless-aware presence is whole, complete and contains all. This is too vast to even think about. When one enters into the portal of NOW beyond time, one has access to all levels of existence. This is attested by enlightened masters.

I'm interested in the practical side of living life. Why should I bother with the difference of thought and Awareness?

It depends upon what you want in life. Please remember that if you want lasting peace and happiness, you have to know the nature of Awareness as different from thought. Everyone wants happiness because it is their true nature.

Happiness is the Aware-Presence itself. It is the truth of being. If you miss out on this one great truth, you miss out on life and can never feel the fulfillment of who you are.

You may succeed by being moderately happy with a million dollars and a good comfortable life, but what happens when you lose it or something happens to it? Loss is nature's way of teaching us what truly matters, to face fears and to grow in our knowing of the eternal nature.

If you have this need for practicality, chances are you are still young and worldly but life has a way of catching up with you whether you like it or not.

We can't escape the truth, which is oneness (Awareness). Eventually you'll discover that what is true is NOT a choice, for without Truth there is only the false, the painful, the suffering, the ignorance and the illusions of the world.

However, ask yourself what it is you truly want above everything else, and you will discover that behind the desires for money, sex, pleasure and comfort lies the need for feeling happy and inwardly fulfilled. These last two are only lasting when there is the realization of who you are.

Can I ever say that I know all there is to know about thought and Awareness?

As long as you are a person you can never *know*, except conceptually.

However, there is still hope of knowing the difference between thought and Awareness enough to bring peace and inner security. It is to this end that this book is written. I certainly do not know all there is to know about thought and Awareness but

I know enough to have found peace. And, this is what I am offering.

Is all Truth the same?

There is only One Truth and it is called by many names such as God, Allah, Now, Bhagavan, Buddha-mind, pure Awareness, Presence and so on, but it is ONE. Everything else emerged from it. When you understand the difference between thought and Awareness you will also understand that everything you see and experience is divine.

Just in the midst of writing this, I received an e-mail from someone who had not written me for close to a year. He wrote me the following:

"It has been some time ago that I have written to you.

Things have deepened, questions have deepened and now it seems that only one question at this time is most important. And

I know there is no answer (by the mind) to that question. The question is, 'How to let everything be exactly as it is?'

A few days ago, when I was lying in bed, my body went to sleep, but "I" was very awake.

I was able to let everything be, even all kinds of thought. I just said every time, 'let it be...' Everything went quiet...it was a very peaceful experience. It was an important experience because this experience was the answer to my question. In a way, there was no question at that time.

Of course, the next day, I tried to relive the experience, but I couldn't. It is a humiliating thing to see that 'the letting be' is not an act, that it is not something I can do. It seems that I can be only aware, and even that is not an act. It is also sometimes frightening to see how much of my experience (it seems almost everything) I am controlling. And, just to see that is most difficult because the mind is always giving comment, always on the run and what is more difficult, it is very cunning in making up stories (before I know it, caught again in the story. Especially 'judge me' stories.)

I am writing this now to give it "body" to see it more clearly so that I am able to see through it. So that I am able not to judge it, not to judge anything, just to let it be.

By letting the mind be, it can sink into the heart (in the past you wrote this to me, and now I am beginning to understand this, to feel the truth behind this.)

It's funny—the most difficult thing in the world seems to be "let it be." And, at the same time it is the most simple thing in the world. So simple that it is incomprehensible and terrifying for the mind.

Dear Burt, thank you very much for reading this and for always replying to the e-mails I send you. That is an extraordinary gift. Your words find their way, it takes some time (in my case), but there's nothing I can do about it. I try to let them be. Let them be..."

This e-mail touched me even though I get several e-mails daily. It touched me because he is "learning" (to listen) that Awareness is the one unchangeable truth and it is the "doer." Everything is as it is because it can't be any other way.

All we can do is "let it be."

Thought, on the other hand, resists, denies, struggles with and controls what-is. It keeps drawing us to our past conditioning to how things should be; how we expect them to be; how we hope they would be without recognizing that conditioned thought seems to create its own reality and we buy into that so called reality.

Our every desire, thought and emotion actually create, in our mind, a reality of their own. Therefore, the vicious circle of our long process in finding the sole simple truth is this—we judge, compare and think-about according to how we have experienced life (which was according to our belief system).

This pattern of thought is a habit that keeps repeating, bringing confusion, fear, complexity and frustration. This habit can remain a whole lifetime, bringing with it stubbornness, cynicism, closed-heart and quiet desperation.

However, as we persist in inquiring and exploring who we are, gradual awakening glimpses start happening, as in the case of the e-mail above.

Finally we discover that we are NOT our thoughts—they are a conditioned response. We are Awareness itself.

When we ask, "Who is being aware of the thoughts?" "Who am I?" "What am I?" we find ourselves dumbfounded and it is natural when we are honest. The reason is simple enough—there is no person in this *eternal now Awareness* to see what is real.

When everything is taken away from us, that is, every thought, belief, past conditioning and even our personal experiences for just one moment, we glimpse, in that one moment, that all we are is AWARENESS! It is as simple as that! When we realize that Awareness is all there is and appears as thought and the world we experience, then we have glimpsed the difference between thought and Awareness. We have found freedom, clarity and peace.

I answered the e-mail above, and, his response was the following...

"It is wonderful to read your mail and to read the book you are writing (which is this one). It all comes at the right moment and it helps me to be 'vigilant' in discriminating

between thought and Awareness. That 'vigilant awareness' is only possible when there is enough trust in the words of the teacher. I can see that clearly now. It cost me many, many years to start to see the simple truth of what you have written down so clearly in your books. The habits of the mind are so strong, it's tricks so subtle. I used to blame them, but now I'm trying to see the mind as an amazing thing. The blaming of it was also subtle, very hard to see through, tricky.

This evening, I was looking at a fish in my aquarium. I looked very closely. In the mind were thoughts like 'you are still not watching, you are labeling the fish, you feel anxiety, you feel this, you feel that.' I could, for the first time, see the beauty of this fish with all its nice colors and didn't even judge the fish because he often gets aggressive against other fish when it is feeding time. I felt love for this animal and felt intimate with it.

Of course, the mind came in after a while and tried to ridicule it on the one hand and tried to relive the experience on the other hand. But I can see this now. It can't help it, it has been a habit for soooo long. I'll let it be.

Burt, thanks for sharing your book and good luck with completing it. It will be a guide for the sincere searcher and would love to read the rest of it when it is finished."

Since we are Awareness having thoughts, why is it necessary to see the difference before we can see their Oneness?

Our brain is designed in such a way that giving attention to something automatically implies ignoring something else. For example, we see the stars and ignore the space; we read this text and

108

ignore the page; we see the movie and ignore the screen.

The brain is built for survival and so, duality is created. Without duality, Creation is not possible. Therefore, in order to see who it is that exists as you, there has to be the clarity of knowing the difference between thought and Awareness. Thoughts always get our attention first and that's why we make it real. However, what is it that sees the thought? Isn't it Awareness?

Therefore, although the thought seems to come first, it is Awareness that makes it possible that there is a thought. When you can see the difference between thought (what seems to be) and Awareness (which is eternally so), then we can also see their oneness and discover unconditional love.

Thought and Awareness always work together just like your body and its shadow. One is eternally so and is the Real You, the other is a pseudo-self and seems real but isn't. It is this clarity which is the awakened life.

If Awareness is complete why is thought necessary?

Awareness is complete and therefore contains thought within it. Pure Awareness does not need anything other than itself to be what it is. It does not need an object outside of itself to be aware of. Awareness is both the subject/object. It is like your body creating a shadow wherever it goes. The shadow is automatically created. Thought is a natural result of being aware. It is when we see thought for what it is that we discover we are not an object but only appear as such.

However, the unconscious state makes thought to be reality and that's when the danger starts. Every time we identify with a thought, we create a thinker of that thought. This thinker creates its own pseudo-reality and then we wonder why we suffer.

Suffering and identification with thought are synonymous. However, you cannot dis-identify from thought, but you can distinguish thought from Awareness. Thought and Awareness live together like sky and clouds, but yet are different. Clouds come and go, become darker or lighter and often block the light from the sun. Is anything really happening though?

Have the clouds really annihilated the sun or merely blocked it temporarily? When something happens, for a short time only, we refer to it as *nothing happened.*

Thought creates the world we experience. For example, everyone sees the same moon but each one sees it according to their concepts, beliefs, feelings and conditioning. If something is seen as it actually is, it loses its tangibility and solidity, and then it is seen as energy.

Bhagavan Ramana Maharshi says there is only the Self. Is the Self pure Awareness?

YES! Awareness is Self-luminous. It is Self-sustaining, Self-aware. When we use language to describe Self, we tend to split into subject/object (thought/Awareness); the Creator and Creation; the Awareness and its content (thought).

The Self is producing, watching and appearing as the cosmic drama of daily life just as a dreamer produces, watches and appears in the dream.

Once we see the difference between thought and Awareness, we also see their inseparability, their oneness and, as a result, see clearly what is real and lasting and what appears as real and temporary. It's all a divine play.

What makes the Self appear as so many different objects?

The Self enjoys experiencing since its nature is enjoyment, laughter, joy, happiness and creativity. The Self is Self-originating. In other words, it is causeless, unborn, had no beginning and knows no end. Its nature is Awareness, known as Presence.

You can see this when you are fully empty for a few moments and all you see is this boundless aware-space. It is who you are. The body is an appearance of this Self just like the ocean is one and yet it creates thousands of waves on its surface. It is Self-perpetuating.

Every living object has this Self-expression known as freedom and this is why control becomes such an "evil" force. Similarly, when thought (impressions from Awareness) are identified with, there is a loss of remembering of our true nature and you feel lost. In this sense of loss, we create the need for power and control to assert our limited persona (mask). And, this is why we have wars, violence, crime and corruption.

It is all stemming from a feeling of lack (something is missing, I'm not good enough, there is something wrong with me I need to be somebody special). Lack creates the need to have, to possess, to own, control and addictions.

One may ask, "Why does the Self create suffering and war when its nature is love?" We are this very Self and have never been anything else. Another glorious gift given to all human beings is the willingness to see or not see.

We can see we are the Self and automatically forgive every thought and emotion or identify with it as who we are. But then again, are we really suffering, or believing we are through our identification? This is the mystery and wonder of being God and not knowing it (or knowing it.)

You are the Self and everything is okay—imagine the relief and freedom when we finally wake up to what is true and lasting.

You said that the difference between Awareness and thought is the same difference between now and time, and human and being. Can you elaborate?

Only the words and labels differ but they are one and the same thing.

You are a human being and everyone on earth knows that, however, what most people do not know is that both are diverse and yet it is their integration which is awakening.

The human is always a *becoming* process and never arrives. It never arrives anywhere because it is never satisfied and always wants more and more.

Have you ever known a multi-millionaire who was at peace and fully satisfied and happy? It is the nature of human to seek, want, crave, hope, wish, desire and think about it.

The human, when the Being is not awakened, lives in a continual unconscious fog expressed as fear—fear of dying, fear of growing old, fear of poverty, fear of the unknown and always trying to improve, overcome, struggle and seek new answers and ways to be better.

And now, here's the great paradox, this whole search and struggle and suffering is for only one thing—*Being* itself!

When we realize that all we ever wanted in our search for power and control was not money or material gain or even safety and security but Being, we suffer a shock, sometimes a literal shaking up of all our beliefs and then followed by its realization and peace. Oftentimes it takes facing death before we start seeing what is actually obvious.

I have read, very often, in Eastern teachings about killing the ego to find lasting peace and Self-realization. Is that how it works?

We have to understand what killing the ego means and it is all just a play of words because there is no ego to kill but a self-image (the unconscious satan).

Also, if the ego is to be killed, who is going to do it? Do you think that the ego can kill itself? Being does not kill anything simply because it sees no opposite and therefore sees no wrong or negative or fear.

All this fear is concocted by the human side trying to protect, defend and maintain its illusory image because it is all it knows.

Your true nature is Being and therefore you are beauty, love, peace, joy and glory itself right here and now even as you read this. However, all it takes is one single doubt and it creates a fog. In our "growth" process, we do not learn anything; do not attain anything and do not overcome anything—we merely see clearly that all is here and now ALWAYS! There is no other NOW. It is always

NOW! Therefore we do not learn anything but clear the fog from our eyes and wake up to what is obvious. Time exists only for the human part of us and is relative truth. The truth is NOW and is timeless!

Please clarify something—if NOW is all there is and I am beginning to see this—isn't the memory of yesterday and the hope for tomorrow also happening now?

It seems so, but it isn't. The moment you think of the past or future you are in present time. In the present time you can live in the past, in your mind, completely and that's what emotional suffering is! However, now is NOT the present time but its container.

For example, whatever you experience is always in the present time. This present time happens only because there is a container that can contain it all and it is called 'The Timeless NOW!' In this NOW beyond time (that's what LOVE is), all is One whether it is Vancouver happening or on the moon—NOW contains it all! Please reflect on this.

I'd like to go back to what I asked before about killing the ego. So, if the ego is an illusion (the me), then why can't I experience the wonder and glory you talk about?

Just because something is an illusion does not mean you don't believe in it. The power of a magician is not just his tricks but his power to make the illusion seem real. He will never divulge his secret because the moment you know the truth there is no longer the illusion and the magician has lost his livelihood.

Similarly, the moment we see clearly that the ego is an illusion (and honestly see the illusion), then it has no power over us anymore. Therefore, we are no longer subject to being victims.

To see the ego for what it is requires the honest willingness to LOOK (listen). Anything that happens in time is relative to our belief system and NOT reality.

Since the human and being are really one, then can't I live the human life while knowing that I am a Being?

If you fully know that you are a Being then there's no one who can say, "Can't I live the human life?" There is only the Being playing the human role. In knowing you are a Being first, you may act fully human in your daily life in all ways such as expression, sexuality and seeming emotional ups and downs, but in truth, you are being lived and have found peace. You see the dream clearly.

The integration of human and Being is the ideal marriage for happiness, peace and fulfillment. This also means that total acceptance of your humanity just as it arises.

Can you map out the way to live the spiritual life?

120

I would never even dream of giving you such a map. The map is not the territory any more than the words here in text are the Truth. They are pointers and you still have to find out for yourself.

There is no map, no specific path or route that one should take except to listen to your own heart. Do not listen to anyone except to FEEL it in your own heart and see its possibilities. Keep open in your heart and LISTEN.

Your own way will be shown clearly when you are sincere in trusting Being. There is no road that is ready-made, let alone a map that will describe the road. The road itself comes into being in the actual walking.

I feel confused when I read material about NOW and TIME without a specific goal or step-by-step guidelines. It seems all so vague!

I can fully understand your feelings as I have certainly been there. In fact, I don't know of anyone who hasn't felt the same way. It is all part of the journey.

The Direct Path is the experience of letting-go, of radically abandoning any identification with knowing anything. Being means acceptance, love, here-now, silence, empty-mind, letting-go, surrender, listening. It is the way of seeing that all fear, fog, anxiety, unhappiness and suffering is a guide towards your thinking. Listen to your internal dialogue (what you are telling yourself is true) and you will begin to see clearly what you have hypnotized yourself into seeing.

After all, the world you experience is all in your mind—this is a fact that has to be accepted if peace can be experienced.

I know that acceptance is essential and my question might seem silly, but if I am to be

honest with you I have to say, "I don't know how to accept."

The word *acceptance* is very powerful and your question is honest and quite beautiful. Acceptance is the death of the ego since ego thrives in resistance; struggle, denial and escape since these are ways the ego uses, which never work but bring greater suffering.

Acceptance is not something that the ego (me) wants to do and that's why it resorts to anger (control). Therefore, can you accept yourself while in the throes of ego? Of course not, however, you can do the steps outlined in this book.

The moment you become aware of anything uncomfortable such as fear, guilt, shame, fear or even attachment—pause for a moment and acknowledge the feeling in your body.

Take a deep breath and then visualize what this feeling in your body would look like (or what color it emanates). Do not label it fear or anxiety, etc.

Then stay with the feeling and if a story starts forming around it such as, "I could have punched them in the face," or "I wonder what's going to happen from this?" etc., then be aware of it and get back to LISTENING to the feeling in the body until it shifts and changes to a neutral feeling.

This is very powerful and the ego will start to die from this simple process.

When Jesus said, "Take no thought of the morrow, let the morrow take care of itself." Wasn't he saying the same thing about being here and now?

Yes, but he was saying so much more. When we focus on the present moment, we are also creating solutions for whatever is ailing us at the moment by simply not worrying about it. When we worry, we block our listening receptivity, our attunement to the universe and lose our balance—that is, get out of sync with the flow of the universe.

When we consciously accept whatever is in the now, we are also creating a flow of abundance in whatever is needed as money, solutions, answers or whatever.

Every time we accept a painful experience and trust that it will work out, then it will work out as inevitably as the sun rises at dawn.

Isn't the world we experience according to how we created it?

Exactly! The journey is a creative experience and it follows the law of attraction, which is, the powerful law of the mind (thought).

When we do not know the difference between thought and Awareness, we still create, however, it is an unconscious creation based on conditioned beliefs and that's how separation creates conflict, struggle, war, pain and ignorance.

When, on the other hand, we know the difference between thought and Awareness, we create paradise effortlessly. As we learn to LISTEN through the Awareness of Presence, we are no longer subject to circumstances and how people think.

For instance, if someone is angry at you (where before it could have ruined your day) now, through seeing what is actually happening, you have compassion and understanding.

When we see clearly the difference between thought and Awareness, we also see the creative process and how oneness (thought & awareness as one) is creating the world we experience moment-to-moment. There is no good or bad, everything is moving according to oneness. Oneness is unconditional Love.

PART II

15

A Simplified and Practical Way

to Awaken Love & Freedom

What you are looking at right now could be just what you need. Imagine your heart warm and open, your spine pleasantly tingling. You feel like floating on air. As you look, the colors are brighter, the sounds clearer, like you are truly experiencing your surroundings for the first time.

This is how you'll feel when you release the "holdings" of your conditioning. Part II will help you, with a pleasant set of exercises, do just that.

I receive several e-mail questions a day worldwide and most questions fall into two categories. First, are personal problems ranging from emotional pain to relationship conflicts.

Second, are the questions dealing with spiritual Truth. This book is an inspired work and the result of many days asking for inner guidance for greater clarification of this most important understanding: the difference between Awareness and thought, and how, through seeing each clearly are seen as one.

All questions about spiritual reality are answered by knowing the difference between awareness and thought. The following exercises will bring understanding through direct experience rather than intellectual comprehension.

Awaken to Love & Freedom is divided into three central chapters. Please do not jump around, but wait for the next step. Each step is geared for its next one. Only when it is completed we start awakening our intuitive heart.

The three chapters are:

1) UNDERSTANDING — What are ego, feelings, emotions, and how they fall into the category of Awareness and thought. How unconscious guilt is in everyone who feels like a separate individual.

2) KNOWING — Your feelings and learning to release them. How ego resists rising above the first six egoic feelings.

3) LISTENING — Learning to listen with your sense of hearing and seeing. How listening alone awakens true nature of peace.

16

Understanding

Ordinarily, we attempt to understand with the daily intellectual mind. We do not yet recognize that the mind that asks questions cannot answer those same questions.

We can only find concepts and beliefs based on our past conditioning. Therefore, we need to go deeper within to uncover questions that the mind asks. This requires not only a form of discipline and know-how but also the courage to do so.

In my experience, I have seen hundreds of people who understand intellectually the concept of oneness, love, eternity and egolessness, but when it comes to living such knowing, it is as if they are babes in the woods.

Most spiritual seekers get the idea that to awaken they have to follow some belief system and then end up knowing the words of that particular system without heartfelt recognition.

What I am offering here is not a belief-system but direct experience when there is sincerity in the heart to find freedom, love and peace. The exercises are simple and enjoyable, but most importantly, they activate the heart's intuition. When you change yourself from the inside-out, the changes are permanent.

What is ego?

The ego is not a solid fact, but a conditioned one. It is the belief that there is a separate life. There can be no lasting happiness, peace, joy nor true love, until the egoic idea drops from direct seeing that it is just a belief.

Most of us have built our ego life during our teenage years and thus beliefs have become solid holdings in our center. The word *holdings* refers to anything that we hold onto and believe to be real. This conditioned state becomes our self-image.

This self-image, which is just imagination, is the ego. The ego cannot love and it carries with it a sense of guilt, so unconscious, that most people have no idea of it.

This feeling of unconscious guilt can be subtle or obvious depending upon your circumstances in life and conditioned past.

This guilt feels as if you are missing something or that you are not good-enough or even the feeling as if you are being bad or done something wrong. It is a nagging feeling, like having a pebble in your shoe and don't know how to remove it.

When the guilt is released through the exercises in this booklet, we start feeling alive again. To be happy and alive does not require being richer or have greater material gain or be smart or become younger. You'll feel alive and joyous because that's your natural state beyond ego—believe it or not.

Most people have taken their suffering for granted as if it is part of Life. We are NOT victims of our emotions and various feelings because, in truth, we are more than a body/mind organism.

What are feelings?

Feelings are energy. All is energy. Energy is the very intelligence of life. Our ability to feel emerges from Awareness.

Awareness is every human being's function and is ONE. You are a human being. There are over six billion humans on this earth.

However, there is only One Being. This One Being is referred to as AWARENESS. Your Awareness and my Awareness are one and the same. On the other hand, what you are aware of is THOUGHT.

This thought is what separates us and makes it difficult for us to know our oneness and love nature. Thought is creative and the world we see in all its totality is a creation of thought (mind). Thought can make or mar our life.

What you believe and think makes up your world of experience. If, through grace you realize you are pure Awareness, then thought will no longer control you and you become master.

This is called awakening.

Our thoughts are felt as a feeling without recognizing they started out as conditioned thought (a mental picture). This type of feeling is known as emotion (e-motion) or motion of energy.

Therefore, pure feeling or seeing, knowing, recognizing, intuition are our true nature of Awareness. When pure feeling is combined with thought, we have emotion.

Our body/mind work together. For instance, if you feel physically tired and you don't feel well, chances are you feel irritable, or reactive. If you feel physically well, chances are you feel happier. Similarly, when you feel clear in your head, inspired and touched by beauty such as love then your body regains energy.

Nine Feelings

Inherent in all of us are nine feelings. Six are emotional and three are spiritual. The spiritual ones are the natural state of NOW Awareness often blocked by resistance created by unconscious guilt.

When this guilt (six emotional states) are released (forgiven) then we unshield what has always been here, known as the three spiritual *now* feelings.

The six emotional states that result from unconscious guilt are: apathy, grief, fear, lust, anger and pride (making up our unconscious guilt.)

The other three make up our open heart of courage, acceptance and peace.

Each emotional state leads to the other as energy increases.

These emotions fall along a gradient scale of energy and action. In apathy, for instance, we have almost no energy available to us and take little or no external action. Our energy increases slowly when we reach grief. Each successive emotion in this scale, all the way up to peace, has more energy and affords us greater capability for outward action.

Remember that emotions are just energy and they can be shifted and changed just by a thought.

As you learn in the following exercises to release guilt, which is a holding in our center, we move to the next and the next until peace is experienced. Therefore, as you let go of apathy, grief, fear, lust, anger and pride, you'll be uncovering automatically the higher energies found in pure Awareness, which are the real

you that has always been here.
Your whole life will turn around
as a result. Everything will get
easier for you.

Please be aware that this turn-around might not happen suddenly. It might be a very gradual process depending upon your drive for truth of your being.

Here's a guarantee and it is this that every time you work through the process of releasing, no matter where you start out—whether in apathy, grief, fear, lust, anger or pride—you'll find that you'll gravitate naturally towards courage, acceptance and peace—qualities of pure Awareness *feeling*.

1) **APATHY**: When we experience apathy, we feel as though desire is dead and it's no use. We are helpless and hopeless and no one can help. We feel dense and heavy and see no way out. Our minds can get so noisy that we feel numb. It is

as if Awareness has completely left us. We have hardly any energy to cope with living and only see failure.

Here are other feelings associated with apathy:

Bored, cut-off, dead, defeated, depressed, despair, discouraged, disillusioned, drained, futile, hopeless, humorless, indecisive, invisible, lazy, loser, lost, negative, numb, overwhelmed, resigned, powerless, stoned, too tired, unfeeling, unfocused, what's-the-use, worthless...

Now take a few moments and remember the last time you experienced apathy. Could you release it if you wanted? Would you have wanted?

2) **GRIEF**: When we experience grief, we want someone else to help us because we feel we can't do anything on our own. We hope someone else can. Our bodies have a little more energy than in apathy, but the energy is so contracted that it is painful. Our minds are a little less cluttered than in apathy, but they are still very noisy and

vague. We picture our pain and loss, often getting lost in these pictures. Our thoughts are completely self-occupied with hurt and whether someone can help us.

Words that describe grief:

Feeling abandoned, abused, accused, ashamed, betrayed, despair, distraught, forgotten, embarrassed, heartbroken, inconsolable, misunderstood, mourning, melancholy, nobody cares, pity, rejected, tormented, tearful, tortured and torn, unwanted, wounded, vulnerable...

3) **FEAR**: Here, we are focused on specific fear since all negative emotions are fear-based. When we experience specific fear, we want to strike out, but we don't, because we think the risk is too great. We believe we probably get hit harder. We want to reach out, but do not because we think we'll get hurt.

Our bodies have a little bit more energy than in grief, but the energy is still so contracted that it is mostly painful. Feelings can rise and fall very rapidly. Our mental pictures and thoughts are about doom and destruction. So all we think about is how we can get hurt and how to protect ourselves.

Other words for fear are:

Anxious, apprehensive, cautious, cowardice, defensive, distrust, doubt, dread, evasive, foreboding, horrified, hysterical, inhibited, insecure, irrational, panic, nervous, paranoid, paralyzed, shaky, secretive, highly self-conscious, suspicious, threatened, trapped, timid, uncertain, want to escape, worried, wary...

4) **LUST**: When we experience lust, we desire possession. We are WANTING. We hunger for money, power, sex, people, places, things, but with hesitation. Yet, paradoxically, we have an underlying feeling that we cannot or shouldn't have.

Our bodies have a little bit more energy than in specific fear. It is still contracted, but the sensations now are sometimes quite pleasurable especially compared to the previous three.

One can indulge in daydreaming about having loads of money or having lustful sex, indulge in pornography or over-eating, etc.

Words that describe lust:

Craving, driven, greedy, exploitive, fixated, gluttonous, hoarding, hunger, I want, impatient, lecherous, manipulative, never enough, controlling, obsessed, possessive, predatory, ruthless, scheming, selfish, voracious, wicked...

5) **ANGER**: When we experience anger, we desire to lash out to hurt and stop others, but with hesitation. We may or may not strike out. Our bodies have a little bit more energy than lust. The sensations can be explosive or intense. Our minds are a little less cluttered than lust, but they are still noisy, stubborn and obsessive.

Our mental pictures are about destruction, and what we are going to do to others. Our thoughts are about getting even, making others pay.

If this energy frightens us, then we lose physical energy and revert back to the experience of lower energy emotions such as apathy, grief, fear in the form of depression, deep sadness, etc.

Other words for anger are:

Abrasive, aggressive, argumentative, belligerent, boiling, brooding, caustic, defiant, demanding, destructive, disgust, fierce, explosive, reactive, outraged, rebellious, resistant, revolted, rude, savage, sizzling, smoldering, spiteful, stubborn, vicious, violent, willful...

6) **PRIDE:** This is common among spiritual-intellectuals who believe they know. When we experience pride, we want to maintain the status quo. We are unwilling to change or move; therefore, we stop others from movement so they won't pass us up. Our bodies have a little

145

more energy than in anger, but it often becomes unavailable.

Although the energy is not necessarily contracted, it is often muted and less visible. Our self-image are about what we have done and what we know. We want others to notice us.

Words that describe pride:

Aloof, above reproach, arrogant, bigoted, boastful, bored, clever, closed, conceited, complacent, critical, dogmatic, false dignity, haughty, holier than thou, hypocritical, icy, unfeeling, isolated, judgmental, know-it-all, never wrong, narrow-minded, patronizing, prejudiced, righteous, self-absorbed, snobbish, stoic, stuck-up, superior, unyielding, unforgiving and vain...

You are Not Your Feelings

Now that we have explored the first six negative emotions, we see that while in their grasp they seem very real. Ordinarily we are trapped into believing this is who we are. It is this belief that has to be released first in our exercises for awakening the intuitive heart.

If you have read this far with attention and allowed yourself the import of what you were reading (as best you could), you probably already feel a little more inwardly relaxed, in touch, and open to your emotions.

If you are not sure, or feel no change at all, don't worry about it. Remember that you are learning a new skill of diligent Awareness. You have had a lot more practice suppressing your feelings and indulging in them than learning to let go of them.

One imperative point here is this—emotions are just emotions—they are the motion of energy set up by our conditioned thoughts and images creating physical sensations. They are NOT you, they are NOT facts, and you can let them go.

The average human being either suppresses emotions in denial of them, and thereby create internal havoc, or indulge in them and get wrapped up in self-pity and victim-mentality.

17

Knowing

Make a commitment. Before you move on to the three positive aspects of your true nature, I recommend you practice releasing of the above six emotions.

Make a commitment to yourself that you deserve freedom from emotional entrapment.

a) Find out how you are feeling right now. Please review the lists.

b) Feel the sensation rather than its story.

c) Locate the point in your body where you feel it most.

d) Visualize a shape and/or color of the feeling.

e) Then visualize the color getting closer to white or light blue. Picture the release as if you have a hard resistant fist becoming gradually an open giving hand.

Rising Above Resistance

(Ego's Major Tool)

In my many years of hypnotherapy practice, I have noticed that most people, even those who were initially honest and sincere, end up resisting the very thing they want most.

Resistance is ego's greatest tool. To win over resistance is to win over ego and awaken what has always been your true vibrant Self.

Have you ever started a project really enthusiastically going at it with fervor and dynamism and then, somewhere along the way, lost the drive?

This is very common especially among seekers. Now, that's resistance. Resistance is quite insidious. It's one of the main things that stop us from having and being what we want in life. In fact, it blocks us from the very thing we are in pure essence.

Resistance comes to us, even when it is something we want to do, simply because we are being told to do it. We hate being told what to do.

> *The more emotionally insecure we are and suffer the first six feelings, the more we resist being told what to do.*

We can't even laugh it off. Our dislike of being controlled is equivalent to our fear of it and so we combat it by being controlling ourselves. Remember that the six emotions we have explored are themselves ego control.

Resistance can be self-sabotaging and counter-productive often creating contradictions. We live in a sea of "should," "have-to" and "must do," and other imperatives. Just know this, when there is an imperative, it automatically stirs up resistance.

Why do we rebel against anything that "has to be?" We feel we have been deprived from our natural freedom of being and so, go about demanding it unconsciously. It is this unconscious demand that stirs up so much reactive emotion, argumentation and conflict.

When you are told you should do something, or you have to do something, what do you feel inside? "Don't tell me what to do!" with a tone that resists saying, "Don't you dare control me." This ego protection often results in the six negative emotions listed. They can be released (forgiven) when there is Awareness in the moment. Our Awareness of what is happening has to come from our choice to stay alert, vigil.

Have you ever said to yourself, "I must work on my taxes?" What happens? You probably resist and procrastinate. We hate so much being controlled that even telling ourselves we have to do such a thing becomes resistance itself.

Yet, here's the paradox, the more we resist, the more we start "shoulding" ourselves. We wonder why things don't get done even though we keep telling ourselves how busy we are and must work. "Should" creates an opposing force equal to, or greater than, the force that you're exerting when you're trying to get something to happen.

Releasing (Forgiving) Resistance

Follow the steps below:

i. Allow yourself to welcome the resistance by inviting it to make you stronger. In other words, accept.

ii. Ask yourself, "Could I let go of this resistance by feeling it and welcoming it? Would I? When?"

iii. Then visualize your "holding" becoming an open hand ready to give and receive.

The Three Rewards

When you start releasing the emotions that you have held-in for maybe years, three other feelings start to arise, hard to pinpoint, because they are spiritual qualities of NOW.

These three qualities are **courage**, **acceptance** and **peace**.

NOTE: These three qualities of courage, acceptance and peace are not attained. They are the NOW itself when we have faced our six "demons" and released them. The release through our conscious choice awakens courage.

This courage not to resist and face our emotional demons leads to acceptance. Then acceptance opens the way to peace.

7) **COURAGE**: Having released negative emotions and resistance, you have automatically also released true courage. We

have enough courage to know we can change anything we want to. We have the courage to face anything. Our mental pictures are those of what we can learn through circumstances in life. We are resilient, flexible and clear. We can support others in the same way. We do not teach others, but help them see through our example of forgiveness (release). We can laugh out loud at our own mistakes and learn from them. Life is fun.

We tap into the energy of courage every time we say *yes* to the release questions.

Words that describe courage:

Adventuresome, alert, alive, radiant, aware, confident, centered, certain, cheerful, clarity, compassion, warmth, confident, creative, dynamic, enthusiastic, loving, open, friendly, focused, giving, happy, humorous, honorable, independent, non-resistant, positive, receptive, good listener, secure, self-sufficient, spontaneous, visionary, willing, supportive...

8) **ACCEPTANCE:** When we experience acceptance, we are able to enjoy anything and everything just as it is. We no longer complain, argue or react simply because we enjoy what-is. We have no need to change anything. It just is, and it's okay. Our body gains even more energy than even courage through acceptance. Our energy is light, warm, friendly and open.

Words that describe acceptance:

Abundance, appreciation, balance, belonging, embracing, empathy, enriched, fullness, gentle, glowing, gracious, intuitive, joyful, magnanimous, mellow, innocent, open, playful, receptive, soft, tender, understanding, wonder, well-being...

9) **PEACE:** When we finally experience peace, we feel whole. Then everything and everyone

is part of yourself. We are all one Being. The body has even more energy than acceptance, but it is more subdued, as inner joy.

The energy is quiet and calm. The mind is clear and empty. Life is as it is and it is okay. Even the intuitive knowing that there is no death arises into our knowing of this eternal now-moment which is timeless.

Other words to describe peace:

Ageless, innocent, young at any age, being, boundless, complete, eternal, free, fulfilled, I AM, Light, Oneness, pure awareness, quiet, silent and enjoys aloneness, timeless, tranquility, whole...

18

Learning to Listen

(Awakening the Intuitive Heart)

Now that you have studied thus far, you have learned about feelings, ways to release them and also learned about the ego's great block to truth known as resistance.

We do not awaken by reading but by practicing the exercises that help us awaken our intuitive heart until we come to know everything written here in a natural way as if saying, "I knew all this in my heart."

The greatest clarity is awakened when we know, clearly and emphatically, the difference between awareness and thought and still see their oneness.

Once you know this truth than all questions are automatically answered.

The difference between Awareness and thought will not be explained further so that we leave it up to you to discover its immense and unlimited knowing through your own intuitive heart.

The exercises here are very simple and even pleasant. Continual practice will bring about inner knowing—a gradual process admittedly but well worth every effort. These exercises merely go beyond mind and into the intuitive heart and that's how recognition starts.

What is the difference between release and forgiveness? *They are ultimately the same.* Quantum forgiveness is seeing clearly that there's nothing to forgive.

Release exercises help you to forgive naturally without any attempt at *trying* to forgive, which doesn't work. However, true forgiveness (or quantum forgiveness) is the only quick way to the realization of your true nature through the dropping of the ego's resistance and fears.

By following the exercises described here, you'll come to know every single thing discussed here in this booklet firsthand through your own inner knowing.

We all want freedom but freedom can only be released from within when our so-called problems are seen for what they are. Most of us have become very good at finding problems and limitations.

Some people are so conditioned to limitation that in every sentence there is some worry or complaint or argument or negative response. This is the loss of freedom and natural joy of spirit. We are experts at the quest for limitation because of our habit of looking for our problems when they are not here. If we only knew that here-now is always fresh new and alive!

The freedom that we inherently are is closer than our next thought. The reason we miss our freedom is that we jump from thought to thought, from familiar perception to familiar perception, missing totally what's truly here and now.

Exercises

Welcome to the following exercises in three parts. The first part is learning to LISTEN to sounds and silence. The second part is LISTENING to sights and silence and the third part is LISTENING to sensations.

1. Allow yourself to sit quietly and become aware of your sensory perceptions. Let's begin with your sense of hearing.

LISTEN to all sounds around you, welcoming every sound without judgment. Do not compare sounds as good or bad. See how many sounds you can hear. Could you allow yourself to listen and welcome whatever is being heard in this moment? Having done so and experienced a relaxed state, go to the second one.

While allowing yourself to continue focusing on hearing, could you also allow yourself to welcome the silence that surrounds and interpenetrates whatever is being heard?

For a few moments, switch back and forth between listening to what is being heard and not heard, including your thoughts.

2. When you feel ready, allow yourself to focus on what is being seen. Could you allow yourself to welcome whatever is being seen, as best you can?

Then, could you allow yourself also to welcome or notice the space or emptiness, that surrounds every picture or object, including (for example) the white space between the writing on this page?

Alternate between the two perceptions for a few moments.

3. Focus on whatever sensations are arising in the moment.

Could you allow yourself to welcome whatever sensation is being perceived in this moment?

Then, could you allow yourself to welcome the space, or the absence of sensation, that surrounds every sensation?

Easily switch back and forth between the two ways of perceiving.

Now, that you have practiced the above for a few weeks daily, you are ready for the following advanced seeing and listening.

Focus on a recent problem or emotional pain and allow yourself to focus on it the same way you did before, to impersonal objects. This is regarded more advanced because it is created by your ego and considered personal.

Could you welcome that memory with all the pictures, sounds, sensations, thoughts and feelings that are associated with it?

Could you allow yourself to notice how most of your experience happens apart from this particular problem?

And, could you allow yourself to welcome at least the possibility that this problem is not as all-consuming as it seemed?

Switch back and forth between welcoming the problem and all its associated perceptions, and then noticing and welcoming what is actually here-now.

* * *

Dear friend, as you do the above daily for a few weeks, you'll find yourself gradually gaining a new sense of clarity and being about your supposed problems and fears, also noticing the exquisiteness of what is already here and now.

ABOUT THE AUTHOR

Burt Harding, founder of the Awareness Foundation in Vancouver, Canada, offers a radical invitation to recognize the truth of our being as already whole and fulfilled.

He reminds us of the love we really are beyond the personal stories we carry. In this way, we come to recognize what we have always known but did not live from—the beauty and wonder of our own true essence.

Burt conducts sessions and workshops in Supersentience, a system devised to help heal deep wounds and promote a shift in the perception of who we really are.

He has conducted studies in higher consciousness for thirty years and had his own television series on the mind/body connection.

Please visit: www.BurtHarding.com

One of the most powerful books on the planet for Awakening Consciousness. Burt Harding offers a radical invitation to recognize the truth of our being as already whole and fulfilled. He reminds us of the love we really are beyond the emotions and personal stories we carry. In this way, we come to recognize how beautiful we really are in our essence. Through Burt, perfection unfolds as it lovingly embraces and lifts you, the reader, to a higher state of consciousness.

www.IntheGardenPublishing.com

CPSIA information can be obtained at www.ICGtesting.com
Printed in the USA
BVOW04s1057241214

380798BV00023B/261/P